HENRY DAVID THOREAU

AMERICAN NATURALIST, WRITER, AND TRANSCENDENTALIST

The Library of American Thinkers™

HENRY DAVID THOREAU

AMERICAN NATURALIST, WRITER, AND TRANSCENDENTALIST

Steven P. Olson

The Rosen Publishing Group, Inc., New York

To the Writing Group, whose spirit carries on

Published in 2006 by The Rosen Publishing Group, Inc.
29 East 21st Street, New York, NY 10010

First Edition

Library of Congress Cataloging-in-Publication Data

Olson, Steven P.
Henry David Thoreau: American naturalist, writer, and transcendentalist/by Steven P. Olson.–1st ed.
    p. cm.–(The library of American thinkers)
Includes bibliographical references (p.   ) and index.
ISBN 1-4042-0504-7 (library binding)
1. Thoreau, Henry David, 1817–1862. I. Title. II. Series.

B931.T44O47 2005
818'.309–dc22

                                                            2005013888

Printed in China

On the cover: Inset: Henry David Thoreau in 1856. Background: A replica of Thoreau's cabin on Walden Pond.

CONTENTS

INTRODUCTION

If a man does not keep pace with his companions, perhaps it is because he hears a different drummer.

—Henry David Thoreau

If you had lived in Concord, Massachusetts, in the middle of the nineteenth century, you probably would have known of Henry David Thoreau. Born in Concord, he returned there after college and lived there the remainder of his life. Among the citizens of Concord, he was considered a bit of an odd fellow who preferred the company of his own thoughts to that of other people. He did not do well with polite chitchat and often irritated his hosts at dinners, teas, and other social gatherings. He never married or had a steady profession. He moved from place to place, living at the Thoreau family home or, at times, in the homes of neighbors while working as their handyman or children's

One of America's greatest writers and thinkers, Henry David Thoreau loved nature and freedom. His most famous work, *Walden; or, Life in the Woods*, covered the time he spent in a cabin on the edge of Walden Pond near Concord, Massachusetts. This drawing from 1854 captures Thoreau around the time of *Walden*'s publication.

tutor. When he became bored with one place, he moved on to another. For two winters, he lived in a cabin beside Walden Pond. To have known Thoreau, you would have had to dig deeper.

Yet, Thoreau had the respect of writer and lecturer Ralph Waldo Emerson (also from Concord); author Nathaniel Hawthorne; publisher Horace Greeley; and a number of leading New England intellectuals. As a young man, Thoreau was invited to gatherings at Emerson's home, where an informal group of intellectuals, ministers, and philosophers called the Hedge Club held meetings. Those attending these gatherings became known as the Transcendentalists. Thoreau proved himself to be a capable thinker. In fact, in later years, he may have been the one who lived his life closest to the group's philosophies. However, of the many people who respected Thoreau, only his brother, John, his mentor Emerson, and his first biographer Ellery Channing could truly say they knew him well.

As a young man, Henry David Thoreau yearned to become a great person, a writer acclaimed for the quality of his thoughts and feelings. Around the time that the Hedge Club formed, Thoreau began keeping a journal. Over the remainder of his life, he filled notebook after notebook with lines by other writers that he fancied as well as his own ideas. These thousands of pages contained Thoreau's original thoughts and

Ralph Waldo Emerson was Thoreau's friend and literary mentor. In addition to being a writer and a lecturer, Emerson advocated a philosophy called transcendentalism, which opposed strict doctrines and emphasized the value of the individual. Emerson and his ideas would make a great impression on Thoreau, and the two men remained close throughout their lives.

feelings, which he formed into the elegant passages that appeared in the pages of his publications.

Thoreau's rich interior life was matched by a robust interest in the natural world. He spent much of his free time by himself in the woods around the village of Concord. Through reading and his own experience, Thoreau acquired a rare understanding of the plants and animals of Massachusetts and their connections with one another. Into this keen understanding of nature's inner workings, he wove his own thoughts and feelings about the philosophical aspects of man. Although Thoreau was often lost among the social customs of the bustling village of

Concord, he was greatly aware of his role as a living creature in nature—a creature who, like nature itself, had a spring, summer, fall, and winter. As many of his contemporaries explored the relationship between the intellectual and the changing American society, Thoreau turned to the natural world for inspiration. In it, he found his personal philosophy.

In his own lifetime, Thoreau did not achieve the fame and respect he enjoys today. He had many critics, including Emerson himself. He struggled to get his essays published in minor periodicals. He was often not paid for his published articles and the lectures he gave at the Concord Lyceum. In the intellectual circles of the Boston area, he was considered to be just a minor follower of the great Emerson.

Yet, Thoreau was far too much of an individualist to be anyone's disciple. Even Emerson scoffed at the idea that Thoreau was simply a younger version of himself. Although neither would deny they shared similar ideas, Thoreau embraced transcendentalist ideas in his own life in a way that Emerson—as a husband, father, pastor, and leader in the community—could not. It took the rest of the world nearly 100 years to recognize the greatness that Emerson saw in his earnest young neighbor.

Later generations have come to appreciate Thoreau's writings in ways that his peers never did. Writers such as Robert Frost and Sinclair Lewis as well as leaders such as Dr. Martin Luther King Jr. and Mohandas Gandhi acknowledged the genius of Thoreau's work. Gandhi once said, "There is no doubt that Thoreau's ideas greatly influenced my movement in India" (as quoted in *Thoreau: People, Principles and Politics*, edited by Milton Meltzer).

Thoreau disliked politics, yet the ideas he expressed in his 1849 essay "Resistance to Civil Government" inspired the civil rights movement of the 1960s in the United States and Gandhi's revolution in India. Thoreau's thoughts on nature greatly influenced the fields of botany (the study of plants), ecology (the science of living creatures and their connections to each other), and conservation (preservation of the environment). *Walden*, his book based on two years of living on the shores of Walden Pond, is now recognized as a literary masterpiece on how to simplify life.

Perhaps his greatest achievement was expanding the philosophy of transcendentalism by living according to the philosophy. As quoted in the introduction to Richard Lebeaux's *Young Man Thoreau*, the first book of his two-volume biography of the author, Thoreau laid down the basics of his philosophical pursuits in his essay "Life Without Principle":

> How can one be a wise man, if he does not know any better how to live than other men . . . ? Does Wisdom work in a treadmill? or does she teach how to succeed by her example? Is there any such thing as wisdom not applied to life?

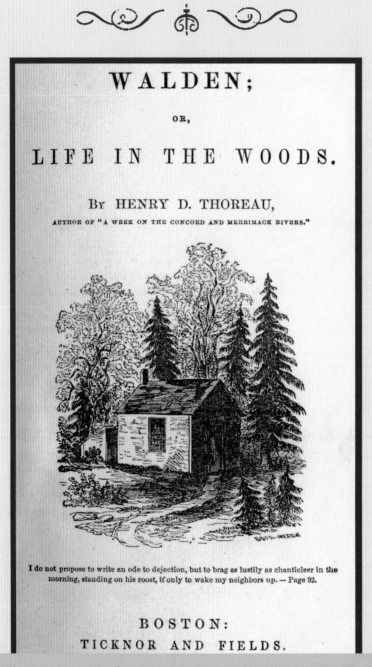

WALDEN;

OR,

LIFE IN THE WOODS.

By HENRY D. THOREAU,

AUTHOR OF "A WEEK ON THE CONCORD AND MERRIMACK RIVERS."

I do not propose to write an ode to dejection, but to brag as lustily as chanticleer in the morning, standing on his roost, if only to wake my neighbors up. — Page 92.

BOSTON:

TICKNOR AND FIELDS.

Walden did not make much of an impact upon its publication in 1854. The book got some favorable critical notices, but it did not sell very well. Although popular success eluded Thoreau, his ideas would go on to influence generations to come. *Walden* is now considered one of the greatest works of American literature.

Thoreau sought a wisdom composed of humankind's breadth of knowledge, his personal intuitions about the natural world, and the experiences of his life. He delivered these ideas to readers in essays that are still relevant today. Rarer still, he lived by those words and pursued a solitary life with joyful energy.

Chapter
1

Forefathers

On July 12, 1817, David Henry Thoreau (who later switched his first and middle names) was born in Concord, Massachusetts. Forty-two years earlier, battles in Concord and its neighbor Lexington signaled the beginning of the American Revolution (1775–1783), which founded a nation in which the rights of an individual are treasured and guarded. That notion of the freedom of the individual proved to be a great inspiration to Thoreau and the Transcendentalists.

By the time of Henry's birth, the small villages of Lexington and Concord had grown considerably in size.

The Old North Bridge, which crosses the Concord River, has been rebuilt many times. It is famous for being at the site of the Battles of Lexington and Concord, the first battles of the Revolutionary War. The Battles of Lexington and Concord would serve as the basis of Ralph Waldo Emerson's famous poem *Concord Hymn*.

The rest of the United States was also undergoing rapid change. The country had fought its first war as an independent nation. When the War of 1812 (1812–1814), fought against Great Britain and various Native American tribes, ended in a draw, it seemed that peace had finally arrived in North America.

Henry was born into what became known in American history as "the era of good feeling," a term that first appeared in the Boston *Columbian Sentinel* newspaper on the day of his

Henry David Thoreau was born in a simple, two-story New England farmhouse. Although the Thoreau family moved frequently, they would ultimately settle in Concord after Henry's father started a profitable pencil manufacturing business. The house, built in the 1730s, still stands on Virginia Road in Concord.

birth. In the first years of Henry's life, the United States began to settle in as a nation. The young country had an identity, a government, and a social structure dominated by the richest families of New England. No longer did America fear invasion from foreign nations. Slavery had not yet become a dividing issue among the majority of the population. For many in the greater Boston area, the era was a time of intellectual, economic, political, and spiritual development.

For the Thoreau family, though, the times were not so good. John Thoreau, Henry's father, was a quiet man who had experienced mixed results as a shopkeeper. His health was not the best either, and for many years, the family moved from rented house to rented house, mostly in Concord, depending on the highs and lows of John's fortunes and health. Henry's mother, the former Cynthia Dunbar, was a devoted mother and wife. A naturally talkative person, Cynthia Thoreau kept active in local charities and the antislavery movement. Despite her active involvement in village affairs, Cynthia managed to provide regular meals for her husband, four children (in birth order: Helen, John Jr., Henry, and Sophia), and any lodgers, guests, or otherwise needy visitors.

Henry's parents shared a love of nature, which was passed on to their children through long walks in the countryside around Concord. Additionally, education was valued in the household. Although John Jr. was considered the more promising of the Thoreau boys, it was Henry who would

John Thoreau found success in the 1820s manufacturing pencils. Henry periodically worked at his father's factory and discovered a process by which to improve the quality of the lead of his father's pencils. Thoreau pencils were considered to be the best of their time and were popular among artists and draftsmen.

become a writer. Although he did not find fame during his time, Henry would become one of America's greatest and best-known writers and thinkers.

EMERSON AND TRANSCENDENTALISM

It is one of the great and happy coincidences of American philosophical history that two of its leading thinkers were from

This undated silhouette is the only image that exists of Thoreau's mother. A loving mother to her four children, Cynthia Thoreau was a forceful personality in the small town of Concord. A committed abolitionist, she was a member of the Ladies' Anti-Slavery Society of Concord and was involved in the Underground Railroad.

Concord, Massachusetts. Although Thoreau produced works that are revered for their original thought, the first intellectual of Concord was Ralph Waldo Emerson (1803–1882).

Emerson was the son of a Harvard College graduate who became a liberal-minded minister at the oldest church in Boston. Ralph, or Waldo, as he preferred to be called, followed in his father's footsteps to Harvard and into the ministry. He was ordained in the Unitarian Church in 1829.

By joining the Unitarian Church, Emerson was already distancing himself from traditional Christian beliefs in New England. During the American Revolution, colonists had given their flesh and blood to the idea of freedom for all. They had created their own country, the United States of America, and intended to form their own traditions, in which all men were created equal. Old traditions, including religious traditions inherited from the Church of England, were called into question. To reflect these changes, the Unitarian Church professed a belief in the moral values of one god, yet it rejected the miracles of the Bible and the idea of the Trinity (a unified Father, Son, and Holy Spirit). Emphasizing rational thought over faith, the Unitarian Church represented an intellectual form of belief in one almighty god. To the Unitarians, God could be discovered inside the individual.

In 1831, the course of Emerson's life changed forever. After eighteen months of marriage, Emerson's wife, Ellen, died of tuberculosis at the age of nineteen. Also suffering from health issues, Emerson began to lose faith in the Unitarian church. He resigned his post, sold his house and furniture, and on December 25, 1832, set sail for Europe in a quest to find intellectual and spiritual guidance. In Paris, France, Emerson visited the Garden of Plants, where scientific methods were used to classify and study plant life. Emerson was so impressed with the power of scientific rationality that he vowed to become a naturalist. Even though his career turned toward literature and philosophy, he was moved to use naturalist ideas in his later writings.

Among the intellectuals Emerson met in Europe, the most influential were the poets Samuel Taylor Coleridge and

Samuel T. Coleridge was an English poet and philosopher best known for his poem *The Rime of the Ancient Mariner*. Emerson was greatly influenced by his work and met Coleridge at a time when the poet was considered to be a "giant among dwarves" by his contemporaries. Although a brilliant poet, Coleridge suffered from domestic problems and an opium addiction. He died in 1834.

William Wordsworth, as well as the Scottish essayist Thomas Carlyle. A few years older than Emerson, Carlyle had been headed toward a career as a Calvinist preacher, yet he, too, lost faith along the way. As a result, Carlyle had begun to cast about for a new relationship between himself and God. Prior to his trip to Europe, Emerson had been inspired by Carlyle's essays in the *Edinburgh Review* and his translation of German writer Johann Wolfgang von Goethe's *Wilhelm Meister*. Carlyle believed there was a light within every person to serve as a spiritual guide; the divine in humankind was within each individual. Neither Emerson nor Carlyle ever lost his basic Christian faith, and both sought to widen their belief in God with philosophy and literature, believing that knowledge of the divine resided in self-knowledge. In part, Emerson's trip to Europe was to meet this like-minded writer, and he developed a friendship and intellectual respect for Carlyle.

On that trip, Emerson also met Samuel Taylor Coleridge, who became perhaps his greatest intellectual influence. A poet, critic, and philosopher, Coleridge was widely regarded among his contemporaries as the brightest of the bright. As a young man, Coleridge had traveled to Germany to study the idealist philosophers Friedrich Schelling and Immanuel Kant. Kant in particular had reacted against the cold rationality of the Enlightenment, developing a more idealistic philosophy that relied on intuition and the senses. In Kant, Coleridge discovered the concept of a transcendental reality within each person. According to the philosophy, a person had inborn yet unknowable abilities to comprehend the exterior world. This greater reality, called a moral law, was a set of principles through which the experiences of one's life could be understood. To the followers of Kant, such as Coleridge, divinity lay within the individual and had to be energetically followed.

In 1825, Coleridge published *Aids to Reflection*, which arrived in America in 1829. Coleridge pushed forward the distinction between Understanding and Reason. In Coleridge's view, Understanding was the rationalization of what was perceived by the senses, while Reason was rooted in the higher, moral perceptions that had been revered by the German idealists and

Thomas Carlyle, seen in this painting, was a great influence on Emerson. Carlyle drew inspiration for his essays and histories from the German transcendentalists and translated works by the German writer Goethe. Later in life, Carlyle alienated himself from his friends and contemporaries by attacking the idea of democracy in his writings. Although Emerson did not agree with Carlyle, the two men remained friends.

other spiritualists for centuries. These ideas and Emerson's conversations with their originators changed the direction of the young man's life.

In the fall of 1833, Emerson returned from Europe with a new wardrobe of ideas. To these ideas, he applied a streak of independence, deeply rooted in his nation's rebellion against Great Britain in 1776. Yet, Emerson was an independent among a nation of independents. He had already distanced himself from the Unitarian beliefs in which he was raised. He began to read Hindu and Buddhist texts and to examine his own religious beliefs as a result. If God is a loving God, Emerson concluded, he would not reject the millions of people who followed the beliefs in these books. God, then, must lie within the individual. This notion, combined with Emerson's strong sense of independence in a vast and untamed continent, were the seeds of the philosophy that would later be called transcendentalism.

On his return from Europe, Emerson began to test his ideas on the lecture circuit. In the nineteenth century, men of learning were often hired by civic groups to deliver lectures on academic subjects and their experiences. For Emerson, and later Thoreau, the lecture circuit proved to be a valuable testing ground, and both writers used live audiences to try out their ideas. Emerson's first lecture, "The Uses of Natural History," was delivered before the Boston Historical Society. It proved to be so popular that Emerson was asked to give the speech

This illustration depicts Ralph Waldo Emerson addressing a large gathering at the Summer School of Philosophy. The Summer School of Philosophy lasted for eleven years and was started by the transcendentalists as a means to share ideas and educate others about their ideas.

quite often that winter. In 1834, he returned to Concord and began to develop more lectures and the material that became his first book, *Nature*.

Published in 1836, *Nature* received little public notice at first, but it represented a call to arms for reformers of poetic and philosophical traditions.

> The foregoing generations beheld God and nature face to face; we, through their eyes. Why should not we also enjoy an original relation to the universe? Why should not we have a poetry and philosophy of insight and not of tradition, and a religion by revelation to us, and not the history of theirs? Embosomed for a season in nature, whose floods of life stream around and through us, and invite us by the powers they supply, to action proportioned to nature, why should we grope among the dry bones of the past, or put the living generation into masquerade out of its faded wardrobe? The sun shines to-day also. There is more wool and flax in the fields. There are new lands, new men, new thoughts. Let us demand our own works and laws and worship.

Although many reviews condemned Emerson's willingness to turn away from the religious traditions in which he was raised, he began to gather like-minded individuals into a growing circle in Concord.

The Hedge Club

During the 200th anniversary celebration of Harvard College in 1836, Emerson discovered that many of his fellow graduates from the Harvard Divinity School had also been inspired by German transcendentalism. This group began to meet informally at Emerson's house with other intellectuals like Margaret Fuller, Elizabeth Peabody, and Bronson Alcott. Because meetings tended to occur when the Reverend Frederick Henry Hedge was in town from Bangor, Maine, the group called itself the Hedge Club. As these people gained fame in their individual pursuits, newspapers began calling them the transcendentalists.

As the host of these gatherings and the leading light of the transcendentalist movement, Emerson became the center of the Hedge Club. By the fall of 1837, he and Thoreau had become friends. Emerson included his young neighbor in gatherings of the Hedge Club.

These bright young people pollinated the thinking of each other, inspiring what was later called "the flowering of New England." Among the fruits of this group was the *Dial*, the first periodical of transcendental thought.

Over time, however, these meetings grew less and less frequent, and individual members became more involved in professional and personal lives elsewhere. By the mid-1840s, the informal Hedge Club ceased to be.

In the area around Concord, others were experimenting with transcendentalism and putting its ideas into practice. In 1833, the Reverend Frederick Hedge published an essay on Coleridge in the *Christian Examiner,* which introduced the ideas of transcendentalism to an American audience. In Boston, Bronson Alcott (father of author Louisa May Alcott) started the Temple School, a first attempt at transcendental education. One of the Temple teachers was Margaret Fuller, who later hosted a series of female-oriented "Conversations" to stimulate support for equal rights for women in New England. Fuller later served as first editor of the *Dial.*

Into this gathering ground of reform-minded individuals, Emerson introduced Thoreau, his young Concord neighbor. As Walter Harding notes in *The Days of Henry Thoreau*:

Perhaps Emerson's greatest contributions to Thoreau— and his contributions both intellectual and material were many—was that he kept wide the horizons that Thoreau had found opened for him at Harvard. Emerson opened his large personal library to his young friend, who made regular use of it for the rest of his life, finding many volumes there important in his development that he could not easily have found elsewhere—in particular Emerson's copies of the various translations from the Oriental scriptures [books about religious belief from Asia].

Although Emerson included Thoreau in this energetic world from its earliest days, the seeds of Thoreau's greatness had already been sown. Thoreau's accomplishments in subsequent years would prove to be a strong match with those of his contemporaries.

CHAPTER 2

BUILDING A LIFE IN OPPOSITION

Even at a young age, Henry Thoreau began to show signs that his life would not be like that of others. As a boy, Henry often did not involve himself in children's games. In *The Days of Henry Thoreau*, Walter Harding describes Thoreau among his classmates:

> Although Thoreau was by no means a poor scholar, many of his classmates considered him "stupid" or "unsympathetic" because he would not join in their games. They could not recollect his ever playing with them, for he preferred to

This hand-colored lantern slide depicts Walden Pond as it looks in the autumn. Thoreau was greatly inspired by the natural beauty of Walden, which he wrote about extensively in his journal. Thoreau was most at home in the outdoors, far away from the civilized society that he often criticized in his writing.

stand on the sidelines and watch. He was so quiet and solemn that their favorite nickname for him was "Judge," but when they wanted to tease him, they called him "the fine scholar with the big nose."

Henry stood out, especially in comparison to his older brother, John. Although their personalities were quite different, Henry and John were close companions and enjoyed hiking through the woods around Concord. Long afternoons were spent paddling on nearby ponds and the Concord River and, before Henry gave it up, hunting game with rifles. Although Henry was quiet, John was more outgoing and carried the personality of their amiable father. A bright boy, John was not as deeply serious as Henry in his pursuit of learning, however.

In the fall of 1828, Henry and John enrolled at the Concord Academy for a tuition fee of $20 each per year. Although the fees were steep for the family, Cynthia Thoreau felt it was important that the boys acquire the best possible education. Sometime in his first or second year at the academy, Thoreau submitted what is now known as his earliest essay, which begins:

The Seasons

Why do the seasons change? and why
Does Winter's stormy brow appear?
Is it the word of him on high,
Who rules the changing varied year.

The Concord Academy, located on Middle Street in Concord, used to stand on Academy Lane. It was moved in the 1850s. The cost of labor was high in the nineteenth century, and it was cheaper to physically move a building than to demolish it and build a new one in another location.

At a young age, Thoreau demonstrated an interest in the natural world and the changing of the seasons, which continued into adulthood. In the introduction to *Young Man Thoreau*, Richard Lebeaux noted:

I was struck over and over again by just how seriously and freshly he regarded the seasons, and natural phenomena in general, as a means by which to comprehend and characterize his own life and human life, and as a medium through which to communicate his thoughts, feelings, moods, and vision.

Thoreau's childhood experiences in the woods around Concord molded the man who formed his personal philosophy within the natural world.

HARVARD YEARS

Thoreau's final months at Concord Academy were spent building the first of his many rowboats. He was not terribly interested in going to college; he thought he might be better served as a carpenter's apprentice. However, his mother was intent on one of her sons getting an education. Thoreau took the entrance exams for admission to Harvard in the summer of 1833 and barely passed.

At the time, Harvard College (now Harvard University) covered a small part of its current campus, and wooded areas were nearby. Despite the demanding curriculum, Thoreau had enough free time to explore the fields around the campus. Thoreau liked to walk down by the Charles River to observe the wildlife that managed to exist in the realm of humankind. His walks extended farther and farther from campus, and on more than one occasion, he hiked the 15 miles (24 kilometers) home to visit Concord, arriving with blisters on his feet.

William Ellery Channing was a classmate of Thoreau's and one of his best friends. Thoreau and Channing spent a lot of time together, and Channing was one of the only people outside of Thoreau's family who really knew him well. Channing's poetry never became well known, and many of the transcendentalists thought that he did not work very hard on his writing.

At Harvard, Thoreau's interest in languages flourished, and his favorite instructor, Edward Tyrell Channing, spurred Thoreau's performance in English composition to above-average levels. Thoreau later acknowledged that Channing was his first inspiration as a writer. Later, Channing's nephew, William Ellery Channing, became Thoreau's friend and his first biographer.

Thoreau also furthered his education independently through Harvard's vast library. In addition to travel writing, Thoreau had a special interest in English poets, extending back through John Milton to William Shakespeare and Geoffrey Chaucer. Although Thoreau later discredited his Harvard education, he petitioned the college's library to give him access to it after he graduated.

In 1836, Thoreau was forced to withdraw from his spring semester at Harvard due to illness, in what is now believed to have been his first bout with tuberculosis. While he recovered in time to return in the fall, it is perhaps during this time away from school that he made the acquaintance of Emerson back in Concord, who the following year wrote a letter to Harvard recommending financial aid for Thoreau. Details of their first introduction have been lost.

In college, Thoreau established patterns in his life that would remain for the rest of his years. When there were opportunities for agreement, he chose to disagree. As Emerson noted in his speech at Thoreau's funeral service:

It cost him nothing to say No; indeed he found it much easier than to say Yes. It seemed as if his first instinct on hearing a proposition was to controvert it, so impatient was he of the limitations of our daily thought. This habit, of course, is a little chilling to the social affections; and though the companion would in the end acquit him of any malice or untruth, yet it mars conversation. Hence, no equal companion stood in affectionate relations with one so pure and guileless. "I love Henry," said one of his friends, "but I cannot like him; and as for taking his arm, I should as soon think of taking the arm of an elm-tree."

Just as he did in high school, Thoreau spent his final days before college graduation away from campus. In the summer of 1837, Thoreau lived with his friend Charles Stearns Wheeler in a hut on the shore of Flint Pond in nearby Lincoln. Certainly, Thoreau's days with Wheeler on the shores of Flint Pond inspired his later experiment at Walden Pond.

On August 30, the class of 1837 graduated from Harvard. As a student in high standing, Thoreau participated in a panel discussion during graduation on commerce, morality, and philosophy. In his discussion, Thoreau had a few words to say about the "commercial spirit."

Let men, true to their natures, cultivate the moral affections, lead manly and independent lives; let them make riches the means and not the end of existence, and we shall hear no more of the commercial spirit. The sea will not stagnate, the earth will be as green as ever, and the air as pure. This curious world which we inhabit is more wonderful than convenient; more beautiful than it is useful; it is more to be admired and enjoyed than used.

These words note that the intention of life is to live it richly and that the pursuit of riches as "the end of existence" detracts from the real goal. As a young man, Thoreau believed that perhaps a man could work only one day a week and spend the rest enjoying the beauty of Earth. He referred to Earth as

At the time of his death, Thoreau's journal was two million words long. Thoreau recorded all of his thoughts in his journal, which would form the raw material that he would shape for his essays and books. Although he was a great writer, Thoreau had notoriously sloppy handwriting.

"this widespread garden," which is "more beautiful than it is useful." Thoreau sensed that man's desire for financial riches damaged the beauty of Earth.

Years later, Emerson boasted to Thoreau that most of the branches of education were taught at Harvard, and Thoreau reportedly replied, "Yes, indeed, all the branches and none of the roots." However, Harvard was an important part of both philosophers' development, as it broadened their views of the world, exposed them to other promising students and great intellectuals, and added a common bond to their friendship.

THOREAU'S JOURNAL

With college behind him, Thoreau set about to establish a career for himself. Like his brother, John, and older sister, Helen, he first attempted to secure a position as a school-teacher, yet he had limited success. In his second week at the Center School in Concord, he resigned in protest over the school's policy of spanking children.

In September 1838, Henry and John opened their own school out of the family home. They called it the Concord Academy, and it eventually swelled in size to twenty-five pupils. As teachers, John was favored for his pleasant personality, but the children were impressed by Henry's knowledge of the natural world. Students learned about nature by rowing boats on the ponds and through frequent walks in the woods. The children were encouraged to turn over rocks, probe the sap of trees, and examine the wildlife living at a pond's waterline. It wasn't until the twentieth century that the principles of learning by doing advanced by the Thoreaus became accepted in the classroom. In 1841, the Concord Academy was forced to close due to John's illness.

As Thoreau struggled to make a career as a schoolteacher, he began with little fanfare what became his life's major effort—journal writing. Perhaps inspired by his friendship with Emerson, Thoreau bought a notebook in the fall of 1837. On October 22, he made his first entry: "What are you doing now? Do you keep a journal? So I make my first entry to-day." With these few words, Thoreau planted the seed of a journal that would grow to two million words across 7,000 printed pages. He copied lines from books that he appreciated into his journal. On those private pages, he also began to formulate his original ideas in the form of short sayings. Much of his professional writing arose from the journal. In his biography of Thoreau, Walter Harding notes:

> From the very beginning it is obvious that the Journal was the result of a professional concern with writing as an art. He discussed therein frequently and often at length how to write effectively, how to edit, how to revise. What is more important is that he used this journal as both a providing ground and a storehouse of materials for his later essays and books.

Thoreau's journal notebooks, along with other works, were compiled into twenty published volumes after his death in 1906.

CONCORD LYCEUM

In 1829, the town of Concord organized a lyceum for its citizens. As the population of the United States began to spread away from major cities, lyceums were formed in small towns to provide public education and cultural events to residents who might otherwise be isolated from them. Started in the 1820s, the lyceum movement grew into a sizable circuit for public speakers.

The Concord Lyceum became one of the largest and best of the American lyceums. Among the hundreds of lectures delivered to the townspeople of Concord were verbal essays

The Concord Free Public Library was founded in 1873 and contains an extensive amount of information about the town of Concord and its many famous residents. The library houses some of Thoreau's original writing, including many of the land surveys that he did and some of his original surveying equipment. Thoreau surveyed dozens of plots of land over the years as a way to supplement the income he received from his father's business.

on morality, history, geology (study of the earth), botany, and ornithology (study of birds)—all topics that captivated Thoreau. After returning to Concord from Harvard, Thoreau became involved in the affairs of the lyceum.

On April 11, 1838, Thoreau delivered his first lecture, "Society," before the lyceum at the Masonic Hall. According to the Walden Woods Project (www.walden.org), Thoreau said: "Society was not made for man . . . The mass never comes up to the standard of its best member, but on the contrary degrades itself to a level with the lowest." Thoreau continued his lecture to point out the meaninglessness of his neighbor's pride in his "clay houses, for the most part newly shingled and clapboarded, and not unfrequently [sic] with a fresh coat of paint." At the age of twenty, he had already begun to distance himself from the people with whom he grew up. In his life, Thoreau took only what he needed from society and gave it only what he valued: the fruits of his gardens, manual labor for his friends and neighbors, and lectures at the lyceum.

The lyceum elected him as its secretary in the fall of 1838, and he later became its curator, holding both posts until December 1840. Thoreau did not return to the lyceum's lecture podium until 1843, when Emerson, as curator, invited him to deliver a Thanksgiving speech. Over time, Thoreau became a more frequent contributor to the lyceum, and a pattern developed for exposing his ideas to a wider audience. His journal was the initial testing place of his thoughts, and the quality of these thoughts improved over time. Later journal entries contained more fully formed ideas, which were introduced into the world via the lecture podium. From his lectures, Thoreau refined his works into essays for publication.

As a speaker, Thoreau was not easy on his audience. His biographer Ellery Channing noted that he had a strange pronunciation of the letter *r*. His voice and delivery were not musical or easy on the ears. And the content of his lectures was not intended to entertain. After giving his "What Shall It Profit?" speech in 1855, Thoreau noted in his journal: "Many will complain of my lectures that they are transcendental . . . If you wish to know how I think, you must endeavor to put yourself in my place. If you wish me to speak as I were you, that is another affair." The effort that he put into developing his lectures, he believed, earned an audience's attention and effort to understand what he was presenting. He did, however, become better at reaching audiences, or perhaps they grew to understand him. His final lecture at the Concord Lyceum, called "Wild Apples," was delivered on February 8, 1860, with an immediate, positive response.

THE PATH ALONE

The rise of the transcendentalist movement in America and Thoreau's personal development in it resulted from the gathering of bright people around his neighbor Emerson. By

Emerson's home in Concord became the meeting place of the Hedge Club, a group of intellectuals interested in trancendentalism. Although he hosted the meetings at his house in Concord, Emerson was not the head of the club. The club had no leaders, it did not have a steady membership, and it kept no records.

meeting people such as Bronson Alcott, Margaret Fuller, and Nathaniel Hawthorne, Thoreau was able to continue an intensive education long after college, while maintaining his independent and self-directed style of living. Although Thoreau is considered to be a direct disciple of Emerson, the movement's principles of self-reliance allowed Thoreau to be both a member of a group and a profound individualist; any group in which he was expected to accept someone else's values as his own would not have appealed to him. It was, in essence, the best of all worlds for him. Given the way his life unfolded and how his personality developed, this coming together of so many positive influences contributed greatly in turning a solitary, thoughtful man into a skilled writer celebrated around the world.

By the time he reached adulthood, Thoreau viewed himself very much as an individualist. In Harding's *The Days of Henry Thoreau*, Thoreau described himself in an autobiographical sketch, of which only a fragment remains:

> I am about five feet 7 inches [1.7 meters] in height—of a light complexion, rather slimly built, and just approaching the Roman age of manhood. One who faces West oftener than East—walks out of the house with a better grace than he goes in—who loves winter as well as summer—forest as well as field—darkness as well as light. Rather solitary than gregarious—not migratory nor dormant—but to be raised at any season, by day or night, not by the pulling of any bell wire, but by a smart stroke upon any pine tree in the woods of Concord.

Others described his erect posture, the long length of his stride, and the large shape of his nose. However, Thoreau's description of himself very soon shifted to how his personality fit in the natural world. As one who faces "West oftener than

East," he was at age twenty-two already looking away from teeming population centers like Boston on the eastern shore. It wouldn't be long before Thoreau found the solitude that he was seeking.

CHAPTER
3

EARLY WORKS

Thoreau's first published creative work appeared in 1840 in issue number 1 of the *Dial*, the periodical started by his transcendentalist friends. His submission, a poem titled "Sympathy," was written about Edmund Sewall, a young friend whose free and pure spirit Thoreau admired. However, there were tensions between Thoreau and Margaret Fuller, the first editor of the *Dial*. She rejected several of Thoreau's later offerings to the magazine, including an essay about a four-day walk Thoreau took with Fuller's brother, Richard. Gossip of a romance between writer and editor were ignored by Thoreau. Later in life, he was rumored to

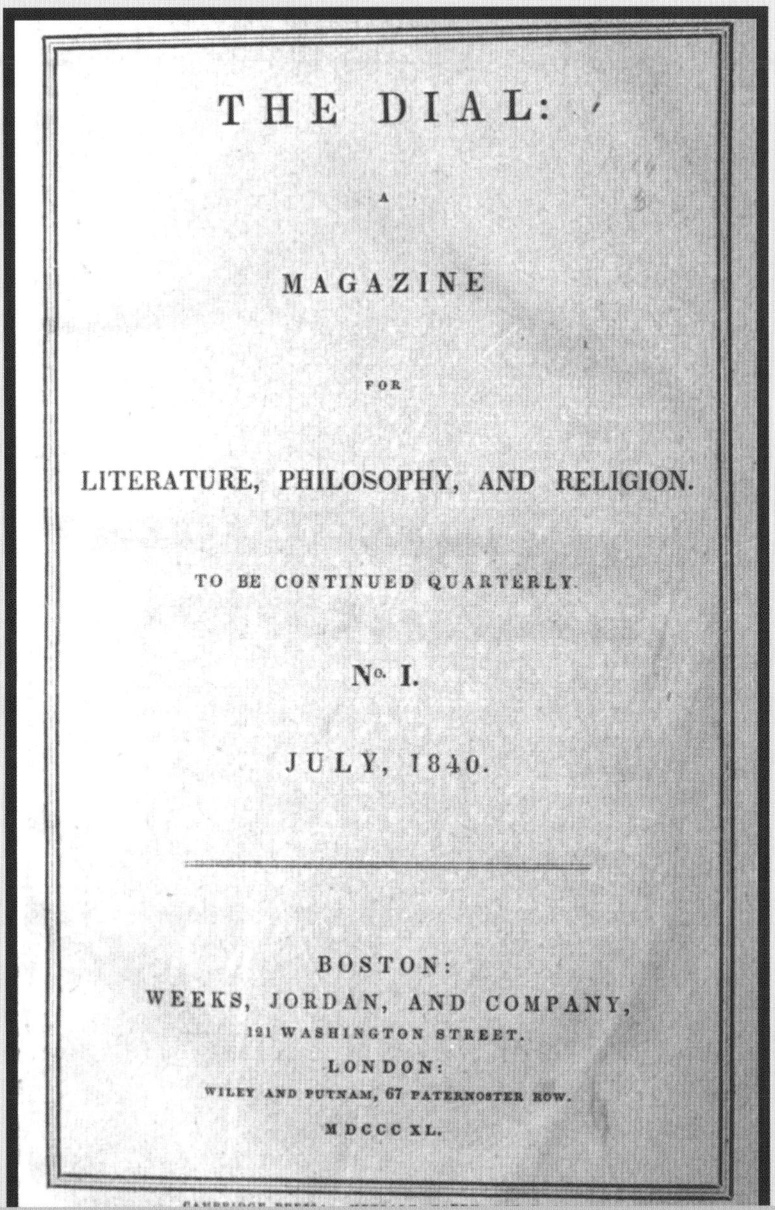

THE DIAL:

A

MAGAZINE

FOR

LITERATURE, PHILOSOPHY, AND RELIGION.

TO BE CONTINUED QUARTERLY.

Nº I.

JULY, 1840.

BOSTON:
WEEKS, JORDAN, AND COMPANY,
121 WASHINGTON STREET.
LONDON:
WILEY AND PUTNAM, 67 PATERNOSTER ROW.
MDCCCXL.

Members of the Hedge Club published the first issue of the *Dial*, which contained Thoreau's first published work, on July 1, 1840. The *Dial* existed for only four years, but during that time, it printed a number of influential articles, poems, and essays, including more than forty by Thoreau.

have said, "In the first place Margaret Fuller is not fool enough to marry me; and second, I am not fool enough to marry her."

Choosing the life of a bachelor, Thoreau turned his attention to writing and long afternoon walks in the woods. According to Walter Harding in *The Days of Henry Thoreau*, he was always well prepared for these walks.

> Under his arm he carried an old music book (his father's *Primo Flauto*) in which to press flowers. In his hand was a cane made of a gnarled stick, one side shaved smooth and its edge marked off in feet and inches for quick measuring. On his head was his size seven hat with a special shelf built inside on which to place interesting botanical [plant] specimens—his brains, he joked, helped to keep the specimens moist.

By 1842, Emerson had taken over as editor of the *Dial*. The magazine published what is believed to be the first of Thoreau's essays on nature, "Natural History of Massachusetts." In it, the earnest young writer begins to draw a hard line between himself and society, clearing the way between himself and the natural world.

> The merely political aspect of the land is never very cheering; men are degraded when considered as the members of a political organization. On this side all

Born in 1810, Margaret Fuller edited the *Dial* from 1840 until 1842. In 1845, her book *Woman in the Nineteenth Century* was published. *Woman in the Nineteenth Century* was a call for female equality at a time when women were seen as second-class citizens. Many of the points that Fuller made in *Woman in the Nineteenth Century* were developed during the gatherings that she held at her house.

lands present only the symptoms of decay. I see but Bunker Hill and Sing-Sing, the District of Columbia and Sullivan's Island, with a few avenues connecting them. But paltry are they all beside one blast of the east or the south wind which blows over them. In society you will not find health, but in nature. Unless our feet at least stood in the midst of nature, all our faces would be pale and livid. Society is always diseased, and the best is the most so. There is no scent in it so wholesome as that of the pines, nor any fragrance so penetrating and restorative as the life-everlasting in high pastures.

In this quotation, Thoreau sees famous American locations such as Bunker Hill, site of an American Revolution battle, and the District of Columbia, the nation's capital, as signs of decay that are connected by a few streets. In comparison, they are always insignificant beside the natural power of one blast of a sturdy wind. Even at the age of twenty-five, Thoreau had already turned away from American society toward the natural world.

During the next twenty years, Thoreau would draw a deeper line between himself and society. He preferred the freedom and spirit of long walks through nature in pursuit of his own thoughts and dreams. More so than any other transcendentalist, he put his beliefs into practice in his life.

John Thoreau Jr. was two years older than his brother, Henry. Henry and John were very close, and the trip they took along the Concord and Merrimack rivers would provide the raw material for one of Thoreau's greatest works. The book *A Week on the Concord and Merrimack Rivers* was published in 1849, after his brother's death. Although it is very highly regarded now, the book sold only 220 copies at the time of its publication.

A WEEK ON THE CONCORD AND MERRIMACK RIVERS

In the summer of 1839, Thoreau and his brother, John, planned a trip together. They would sail down the Concord River, which flowed through their hometown, and then up the Merrimack River as far as they could go. For the trip, they needed to build a suitable boat. Calling their boat the *Musketaquid*, the Native American name for the Concord River, the vessel was about 15 feet (4.6 m) long and about 3 feet (0.9 m) wide. At night, the mast of the boat would be removed, and the brothers would hang the cotton sail from it to make a tent.

By the end of August, Henry and John pushed their boat into the Concord River and set sail on what would become the greatest trip of their short lives together.

Although they left Concord on August 31 and returned on September 13, Thoreau compressed the details of the trip into seven days for his book *A Week on the Concord and Merrimack Rivers*. In the book Thoreau uses the cycle of a week from Saturday to Saturday as a means to describe the cycle of their lives together. As Henry and John prepare to sail the river, Thoreau sets the scene.

> It is worth the while to make a voyage up this stream, only to see how much country is in the rear of us . . . Many waves are there agitated by the wind, keeping nature fresh, the spray blowing in your face, reeds and rushes waving; ducks by the hundred, all uneasy in the surf, in the raw wind, just ready to rise, and now going off with a clatter and a whistling like riggers straight for Labrador.

In these stirring words, Thoreau likened his feelings before the start of the trip to the ducks on the water, preparing for their yearly migration, a long flight north to Labrador Island. There was a restlessness to get going so they could see what was at the far end of the journey. At the beginning of the trip, Thoreau was preparing himself for the changes that were to come.

As the days progressed, Thoreau detected the changing of the seasons from summer to fall. At the same time, the young brothers were migrating through changes in their lives as well. Midway through the week, in the midst of this state of change, Thoreau examined the nature of friendship.

> Friendship is . . . remembered like heat lightning in past summers. Fair and flitting like a summer cloud;—there is always some vapor in the air, no matter how long the drought; there are even April showers . . . The Friend is some fair floating isle of palms eluding the mariner in Pacific seas.

On this trip on these rivers, Thoreau was noting that the friendship between him and his brother had become like a far-off island, or a flash of heat lightning in past summers. Around the time of their voyage, the two brothers had become rivals over the hand in marriage of the same woman, Ellen Sewall. Their boyish friendship had been replaced by an adult competition. Although both were rejected by her, their friendship was changed forever. Just as people change, Thoreau seemed to suggest, the connections between people can change even more. In the transcendentalist ideal, the individual must be true to his inner light and must follow his own dreams. Yet, if two individuals are true to themselves, it is a rare thing that they can be true friends to each other forever. To Thoreau, the notion of friendship was hard to capture and, when it was found, soon disappeared like a summer cloud.

At the end of the journey, Thoreau again turned to the symbol of birds.

> Though the shadows of the hills were beginning to steal over the stream, the whole river valley undulated with mild light, purer and more memorable than the noon. For so day bids farewell even to solitary vales [valleys] uninhabited by man. Two herons, *Ardea herodias*, with their long and slender limbs relieved against the sky, were seen traveling high over our heads,—their lofty and silent flight, as they were wending their way at evening, surely not to alight in any marsh on the earth's surface, but, perchance, on the other side of our atmosphere . . . Bound to some northern meadow, they held on their stately stationary flight, like the storks in the picture, and disappeared at length behind the clouds.

As they approached their home in Concord, Thoreau saw himself and his brother as herons flying onward in the twilight on a journey to "some northern meadow," like the ducks at the beginning of the trip. For Thoreau, the two herons flying side by side was a touching image; less than three years after the brothers' trip together, John died in Thoreau's arms from tetanus that resulted from an infected cut. Starting on Saturday and

Thoreau kept the furnishings of his cabin at Walden very simple. The only furniture he owned during those two years were three chairs, a desk, a table, and a bed. His furniture is now housed in the Concord Museum.

ending on Saturday, the two brothers, as birds, sailed on past the end of their lives together behind the clouds.

Thoreau was devastated by the death of his older brother. With John's death, however, Thoreau realized that his own life had a beginning, middle, and end, and that he had to become more aware of it. In a sense, his brother's death freed him to become what he really wanted to be: a writer who embraced the transcendentalist notion of the self-reliant man. In his

1837 address to the Harvard Phi Beta Kappa Society, Emerson had defined the self-reliant American intellectual. His speech, "The American Scholar," rejected American dependence on European intellectual traditions and defined the three pillars of the American scholar: nature, books, and action. Thoreau would lean on these pillars for the rest of his life, producing literary works that have stood the test of time.

WALDEN POND

By the winter of 1841, Thoreau had still not found the time or the solitude to concentrate on the essay on the river trip with his brother. In his journal, he wrote:

> I want to go soon and live away by the pond, where I shall hear only the wind whispering among the reeds. It will be success if I shall have left myself behind. But my friends ask what I will do when I get there. Will it not be employment enough to watch the progress of the seasons?

Two months later, his brother was dead, and it took another three years for Thoreau to lose himself in the "progress of the seasons." On July 4, 1845, he moved into an unfinished cabin that he had built at Walden Pond, just outside of Concord, on land that his friend Emerson had

Walden Pond was only a few miles from the center of Concord. Although Thoreau's cabin is now gone, the place where it once stood is marked by a pile of stones. Modern visitors to Walden add a stone to the pile before they leave.

purchased to save its trees from being cut down. There, he began to write *A Week on the Concord and Merrimack Rivers* and lived the life that would later inspire his masterpiece, *Walden; or, Life in the Woods*.

The two years that he lived at Walden Pond were a grand experiment in self-reliance in nature. Thoreau grew his own crops, cooked his own bread on an outdoor fire, and continued to build onto his own home. He lived by the labor of his hands—as a handyman and surveyor in Concord, and as a writer in his cabin in the woods. The cabin cost $28.13 to build, and after eight months of living in it, he had spent $8.74 for food, $8.41 for clothing, and $2.00 for the coal to fuel the stove. With a little more than $47, he had provided his own essentials of food, clothing, and shelter. As he later wrote in the "Where I Lived and What I Lived For" chapter of *Walden*: "I went to the woods because I wished to live deliberately, to front only the essential facts of life, and see if I could not learn what it had to teach, and not, when I came to die, discover that I had not lived."

Living no more than a mile (1.6 km) from the center of town, Thoreau was close enough to visit Concord every day, yet far enough to examine the town objectively. Much like holding something at arm's length, he looked at the society from which he came and found it destructive to the quality of someone's life. As he wrote in the "Economy" chapter of *Walden*:

I see young men, my townsmen, whose misfortune it is to have inherited farms, houses, barns, cattle, and farming tools; for these are more easily acquired than got rid of . . . Who made them serfs of the soil? Why should they eat their sixty acres [24.3 hectares], when man is condemned to eat only his peck of dirt? Why should they begin digging their graves as soon as they are born . . . ? How many a poor immortal soul have I

Walden,

or

Life in the Woods.

Addressed to my Townsmen.

By

Henry D Thoreau.

At the time the following
pages were written, I lived alone, in
the woods, a mile from any
neighbor, in a house of my own
building, on the shore of Walden
Pond, in Concord, Massachusetts,
and earned my living by the labor
of my hands, exclusively. I lived
there two years and two months.
At present I am a sojourner
in civilized life again.

I should not obtrude myself
and my affairs so much on

This is the title page of Thoreau's original manuscript copy of *Walden*. Thoreau would revise *Walden* seven times before completing it. Thoreau spent over two years living at Walden Pond, but he compressed the time down to one year in his book. Although Thoreau continued to write for the rest of his life, *Walden* was the last book that he published.

met well nigh crushed and smothered under its load, creeping down the road of life, pushing before it a barn seventy-five feet by forty [22.9 by 12.2 meters] . . .

In his view, the owners of farms and houses are, in turn, owned by their possessions. As he notes later in the same chapter, "Men have become tools of their tools." By carefully identifying the things he needed in food, clothing, and shelter, Thoreau realized that much of what drives men to work so hard is the notion of want. Men want larger houses, nicer clothes, and more and more possessions. Yet, as Thoreau demonstrated in his example of living at Walden Pond, men do not need these things. Philosophically, his approach is Buddhist; a basic belief of Buddhism is that much pain in life comes from desire for things that are not necessary to life. Thoreau applied that idea very carefully to his own life at Walden.

Although Thoreau pursued simplicity and self-reliance, he realized that such a life was not for all. His message in the book is to consider his example, yet instead of following it, readers should follow their own lead. "I desire that there may be as many different persons in the world as possible; but I would have each one be very careful to find out and pursue his own way, and not his father's or his mother's or his neighbor's instead." In a life freed from these material wants, Thoreau was free to explore the natural world.

We need the tonic of wildness—to wade sometimes in marshes where the bittern and the meadow-hen lurk, and hearing the booming of the snipe; to smell the whispering sedge where only some wilder and more solitary fowl builds her nest, and the mink crawls with its belly close to the ground.

This "tonic of wildness" fuels the inner world, providing a creative energy that, in Thoreau's case, led to the most productive period in his life. At the end of his stay at Walden, Thoreau was even a bit surprised at what he had done.

I learned this, at least, by my experiment: that if one advances confidently in the direction of his dreams, and endeavors to live the life which he has imagined, he will meet with a success unexpected in common hours. He will put some things behind, will pass an invisible boundary; new, universal, and more liberal laws will begin to establish themselves around and within him; or the old laws be expanded, and interpreted in his favor in a more liberal sense, and he will live with the license of a higher order of beings. In proportion as he simplifies his life, the laws of the universe will appear less complex, and solitude will not be solitude, nor poverty poverty, nor weakness weakness.

Although the philosopher Immanuel Kant believed that a moral law existed in all human beings, Thoreau found his "new, universal, and more liberal laws" in the natural world. Nature inspired Thoreau in ways that material possessions never could. Although Thoreau's cabin was no more than 15 feet (4.6 m) across, it was his castle in the air. In his pursuit of a simple life freed from want, Thoreau provided a timeless meditation on the role of man in society.

CHAPTER 4

FINDING HIS OWN WAY

After two years at the shores of Walden Pond, Thoreau decided to move back to Concord. Emerson was headed to Europe for an extended lecture tour, and he asked Thoreau to watch over his ailing wife and his children. In the privacy of his journal, Thoreau admitted that leaving Walden Pond may have been a mistake: "Why I left the woods, I do not think I can tell. I have often wished myself back." For the remainder of his life, he struggled to achieve the peace and solitude that he had enjoyed at Walden Pond. Although Thoreau never lived again outside of Concord, he never stopped exploring the natural world and continued to record his thoughts and observations in his journal. While many of Thoreau's friends, including Emerson, grew frustrated with his stubborn personality and his failure to become a respected writer, Thoreau did indeed realize his dreams. As he predicted in *Walden*, Thoreau met "with a success unexpected in common hours."

"Civil Disobedience"

In July 1846, Sam Staples, the constable and tax collector for the town of Concord, stopped Thoreau in the street. Staples informed Thoreau that he needed to pay his poll tax for the last several years. At this time in the United States, a poll tax was a fixed fee paid by all citizens. Eventually, the poll tax became a requirement for having the right to vote. Up until the civil rights movement of the 1960s, the poll tax was used in many states to keep nonwhites from voting. In 1964, the Twenty-fourth Amendment to the U.S. Constitution outlawed the poll tax.

Thoreau refused to pay what he owed as a protest against the government and the Mexican-American War. Even after Staples offered to pay the tax for him, Thoreau suggested that Staples should resign from his post. Annoyed by the suggestion, Staples warned Thoreau that he would have to be imprisoned if he continued to refuse payment. When Thoreau replied that now was as good a time as any, Staples marched him down to jail.

This hand-colored woodcut shows August Spies, a Chicago anarchist who, in 1886, was convicted of conspiracy to commit murder. Spies was a labor activist, but unlike Thoreau he advocated using force in order to bring about change. During a labor rally in Chicago's Haymarket Square, a protester threw a bomb, which killed four policemen. Although Spies was speaking at the time, he and six other men were arrested. They were innocent of the crime, but Spies was sent to the gallows in 1887.

Much to Thoreau's irritation, someone left payment for his years of unpaid poll taxes on Staples's doorstep that night. In the morning, Thoreau was released. Although it was only one night, Thoreau's experience in jail inspired him to write a towering document to the power of nonviolent resistance.

Originally published under the title "Resistance to Civil Government" (renamed "Civil Disobedience" after his death), Thoreau's essay introduced the idea of civil disobedience as a means of promoting change in government by resisting it in nonviolent ways.

Although his actions led to his imprisonment, Thoreau describes his jail cell in surprising terms: "The rooms were whitewashed once a month; and this one, at least, was the whitest, most simply furnished, and probably the neatest apartment in the town." In his appreciation for the clean simplicity of his jail cell, Thoreau returned to a place similar to Walden Pond; in the middle of town, he found a clean and simple place to retreat from the troubles of American society. As he notes in the essay, "Under a government which imprisons any unjustly, the true place for a just man is also a prison."

In the U.S. system of government, the rights of the individual should be held in highest regard, as noted in the second paragraph of the Declaration of Independence:

We hold these truths to be self-evident, that all men are created equal, that they are endowed by their Creator with

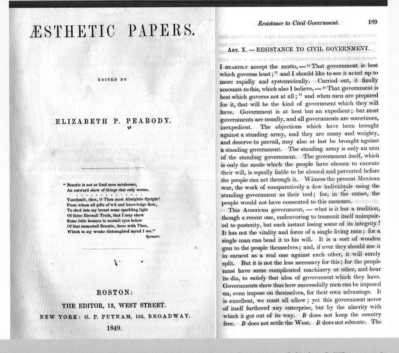

ÆSTHETIC PAPERS.

EDITED BY

ELIZABETH P. PEABODY.

"Beautie is not as fond men misdeeme,
    An outward show of things that only seeme.

Vouchsafe, then, O Thou most Almightie Spright!
From whom all gifts of wit and knowledge flow,
Of thine Eternall Truth, that I may show
Some little beames to mortall eyes below
Of that immortall Beautie, there with Thee,
Which in my weake distraughted mynd I see."
                                        Spenser.

BOSTON:
THE EDITOR, 13, WEST STREET.
NEW YORK: G. P. PUTNAM, 155, BROADWAY.
1849.

Resistance to Civil Government.   189

ART. X. — RESISTANCE TO CIVIL GOVERNMENT.

I HEARTILY accept the motto, — "That government is best which governs least;" and I should like to see it acted up to more rapidly and systematically. Carried out, it finally amounts to this, which also I believe, — "That government is best which governs not at all;" and when men are prepared for it, that will be the kind of government which they will have. Government is at best but an expedient; but most governments are usually, and all governments are sometimes, inexpedient. The objections which have been brought against a standing army, and they are many and weighty, and deserve to prevail, may also at last be brought against a standing government. The standing army is only an arm of the standing government. The government itself, which is only the mode which the people have chosen to execute their will, is equally liable to be abused and perverted before the people can act through it. Witness the present Mexican war, the work of comparatively a few individuals using the standing government as their tool; for, in the outset, the people would not have consented to this measure.

This American government, — what is it but a tradition, though a recent one, endeavoring to transmit itself unimpaired to posterity, but each instant losing some of its integrity? It has not the vitality and force of a single living man; for a single man can bend it to his will. It is a sort of wooden gun to the people themselves; and, if ever they should use it in earnest as a real one against each other, it will surely split. But it is not the less necessary for this; for the people must have some complicated machinery or other, and hear its din, to satisfy that idea of government which they have. Governments show thus how successfully men can be imposed on, even impose on themselves, for their own advantage. It is excellent, we must all allow; yet this government never of itself furthered any enterprise, but by the alacrity with which it got out of its way. *It* does not keep the country free. *It* does not settle the West. *It* does not educate. The

In May 1849, a publication called the *Aesthetic Papers* published Thoreau's essay "Resistance to Civil Government." The essay would later be renamed "Civil Disobedience." "Civil Disobedience" was one of Thoreau's most significant essays, and it would go on to influence leaders such as Mohandas Gandhi and Martin Luther King Jr.

certain unalienable Rights, that among these are Life, Liberty and the pursuit of Happiness.—That to secure these rights, Governments are instituted among Men, deriving their just powers from the consent of the governed . . .

Seventy years after Thomas Jefferson penned the Declaration, however, Thoreau believed that the government had failed in its use of "just powers."

[The American government] is a sort of wooden gun to the people themselves. But it is not the less necessary for this; for the people must have some complicated machinery or other, and hear its din, to satisfy that idea of government which they have. Governments show thus how successfully men can be imposed on, even impose on themselves, for their own advantage. It is excellent, we must all allow. Yet this government never of itself furthered any enterprise, but by the alacrity with which it got out of its way. It does not keep the country free. It does not settle the West. It does not educate. The character inherent in the American people has done all that has been accomplished; and it would have done somewhat more, if the government had not sometimes got in its way.

Thoreau compares the inflexible and threatening U.S. government with the individual man who has kept the country free and begun to settle the West. The spirit of self-reliance that brought so many individuals to the United States has become part of the American character. However, Thoreau argues that the government has stood in the way of this spirit. The spirit of the individual, deeply tied to the transcendentalist notion of self-reliance, has suffered in Thoreau's view. Specifically, Thoreau identifies the U.S. government's greatest disgrace.

How does it become a man to behave toward this American government to-day? I answer, that he cannot without disgrace be associated with it. I cannot for an instant recognize that political organization as my government which is the slave's government also.

In 1846, the conflict over slavery was beginning to rise, and Thoreau's views in "Civil Disobedience" were shared by many of the abolitionists (those who opposed slavery) of that era.

When a sixth of the population of a nation which has undertaken to be the refuge of liberty are slaves, and a whole country is unjustly overrun and conquered by a foreign army, and subjected to military law, I think that it is not too soon for honest men to rebel and revolutionize.

Thoreau underlines some fundamental problems: How can America be the nation that protects freedom for the individual, when a sixth of its population has no freedom? How is it possible that America can be the champion of freedom when it was in 1846 overrunning the independent nation of Mexico in the Mexican-American War? In the pursuit of his own sense of freedom, Thoreau argues that he must make the choice of resisting this government and its old and cruel laws that allow slavery to continue. "It costs me less in every sense to incur the penalty of disobedience to the State [government] than it would to obey. I should feel as if I were worth less in that case."

In closing, Thoreau offers a challenge to each reader, each American, and each human being.

> Is it not possible to take a step further towards recognizing and organizing the rights of man? There will never be a really free and enlightened State until the State comes to recognize the individual as a higher and independent power, from which all its own power and authority are derived, and treats him accordingly.

Through individual resistance, Thoreau notes, the U.S. government can be made to change. It can be forced to live up to the ideals outlined by Jefferson in the Declaration of Independence, so that all people, who are equal under the higher laws to which Thoreau obeys, are indeed created equal under the law of the land.

When the essay was published in the *Aesthetic Papers* in 1849, it was almost completely overlooked. It wasn't long, however, before the issue of slavery could no longer be ignored, and the Civil War (1861–1865) nearly tore the country apart. Although the war did not end the repression of equal rights in America, Thoreau's words did inspire others, years later, to take up the cause again. As the Rev. Dr. Martin

Luther King Jr., leader of the civil rights movement, noted in *The Autobiography of Dr. Martin Luther King, Jr.*:

> I became convinced that noncooperation with evil is as much a moral obligation as is cooperation with good. No other person has been more eloquent and passionate in getting this idea across than Henry David Thoreau. As a result of his writings and personal witness, we are the heirs of a legacy of creative protest. The teachings of Thoreau came alive in our civil rights movement; indeed, they are more alive than ever before.

"A PLEA FOR CAPTAIN JOHN BROWN"

Thoreau was greatly moved by another man's act of resistance to the institution of slavery. On October 16, 1859, Captain John Brown led a group of men, including three of his sons, to raid the armory at Harpers Ferry, Virginia (now West Virginia). His goal was to capture weapons and take them into the South, where he would lead an armed uprising against slavery. Brown's men took over the armory but could not hold it when a group of U.S. Marines stormed the facility. During the fighting, two of Brown's sons were killed, and another escaped. Brown was captured.

Two weeks after Brown's capture, Thoreau spoke at the Concord Lyceum on behalf of the imprisoned man. In "A

John Brown was a Northern abolitionist who sought to end slavery at any cost. Besides his raid at Harpers Ferry in Virginia, John Brown was a part of the Underground Railroad, gave land to escaped slaves, and was a founder of the League of Gileadites, an organization that sought to protect fugitive slaves from being captured and sent back to their owners. This is a photograph of John Brown kissing a young child on the way to his execution.

Plea for Captain John Brown," Thoreau answered those who criticized Brown's actions.

> "Misguided"! "Garrulous"! "Insane"! "Vindictive"! So ye write in your easy-chairs, and thus he wounded responds from the floor of the Armory, clear as a cloudless sky, true as the voice of nature is: "No man sent me here; it was my own prompting and that of my Maker. I acknowledge no master in human form."

Although he may have disagreed with the tactics Brown used, Thoreau was deeply moved by Brown's willingness to act on his beliefs. To Thoreau, Brown answered the higher calling that he found in himself, his own moral law. While Brown's disobedience was not civil in any sense, it was certainly in keeping with Thoreau's belief in individual resistance.

At the end of a weeklong trial, Brown was found guilty and sentenced to death. On the morning of December 2, 1859, John Brown was hanged.

THE MAINE WOODS

In August 1846, Thoreau departed Concord to visit his cousin, George Thatcher, in Bangor, Maine. A lumberman, Thatcher was going to look at some property for his company up the Penobscot River and wanted Thoreau to join him on the trip.

The notes from this trip and later ones were woven into *The Maine Woods*, a collection of narratives that celebrate the majesty of the natural world and the need, now more important than ever, to protect it.

As soon as Thoreau arrived in Bangor, he and Thatcher set off upriver and into the woods of Maine. For Thoreau, the voyage had the added excitement of adventure, for he intended to climb Mount Katahdin, the highest mountain in Maine. But Thoreau knew that men like Thatcher would soon be conquering the forests around it. As Thoreau wrote in the first narrative of *The Maine Woods*: "The mission of men there seems to be, like so many busy demons, to drive the forest all out of the country, from every solitary beaver-swamp and mountain-side, as soon as possible." At the time, Thoreau's words may have seemed silly to his readers. The forests of Maine stretched from the southeast coast to the border of Canada. The interior of Maine was inhabited by a few fur trappers and the remaining members of Native American tribes.

Thoreau wrote of walking and paddling canoes for days without seeing another human being. However, he saw the future had already arrived in Bangor; in 1837, the 250 sawmills in the area "sawed two hundred millions of feet (60,960,000 m) of boards annually." When the trees in the area were gone, men like his cousin Thatcher moved inland, up the rivers like the Penobscot, whose protectors were the few remaining native people. On his first trip, Thoreau noticed a shabby Native American village on an island. On a later trip, it was almost gone.

Thatcher brought along a gun in hopes of hunting a moose. During an excursion with some hunters, the party managed to bring down a large female moose. Thoreau was distressed to see this creature skinned. After the skin had been given to their Native American guide and a chunk of meat stored for their trip, the large and noble animal was left to rot on the ground. Yet these men continued to kill moose, often without using any part of the animal. This irritated Thoreau. As he wrote in *The Maine Woods*:

> But, on more accounts than one, I had had enough of moose-hunting. I had not come to the woods for this purpose, nor had I foreseen it, though I had been willing to learn how the Indian maneuvered; but one moose killed was as good, if not as bad, as a dozen. The afternoon's tragedy, and my share in it, as it affected the innocence, destroyed the pleasure of my adventure . . . But this hunting of the moose merely for the satisfaction of killing him,—not even for the sake of his hide,— without making extraordinary exertion or running any risk yourself, is too much like going out by night to some wood-side pasture and shooting your neighbor's horses.

Maine's Baxter State Park is home to Mount Katahdin, which at 5,270 feet (1,606 meters) is the tallest mountain in Maine. Thoreau climbed Mount Katahdin in 1846. The 350-mile-long (563 km) Penobscot River, shown here as it winds past Mount Katahdin, is Maine's longest river. Thoreau was greatly impressed with Maine's natural beauty.

This mindless destruction of life bothered Thoreau, whose goals on the trip were of a more peaceful nature. As the hunters went off to hunt more moose, Thoreau was left at camp to gather fallen branches and to build a fire. He regretted the afternoon and the future destruction of the woods by lumbermen. As he recounted in *The Maine Woods*:

> But the pine is no more lumber than man is, and to be made into boards and houses is no more its true and highest use than the truest use of a man is to be cut down and made into manure. There is a higher law affecting our relation to pines as well as to men . . . Every creature is better alive than dead, men and moose and pine-trees, and he who understands it aright will rather preserve its life than destroy it.

Philosophically, Thoreau returned to his idea of a higher law, which applies to pine trees, men, and animals. If this higher law is inside each of us, then Thoreau suggests that we must protect the special nature inside each living creature. Thoreau made a grand suggestion in *The Maine Woods*:

> Why should not we, who have renounced the king's authority, have our national preserves, where no villages need be destroyed, in which the bear and panther, and some even of the hunter race, may still exist, and not be

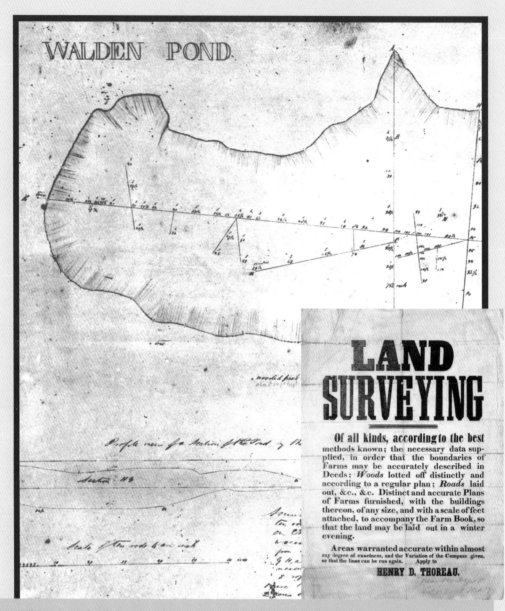

WALDEN POND.

LAND SURVEYING

Of all kinds, according to the best methods known; the necessary data supplied, in order that the boundaries of Farms may be accurately described in Deeds; *Woods* lotted off distinctly and according to a regular plan; *Roads* laid out, &c., &c. Distinct and accurate Plans of Farms furnished, with the buildings thereon, of any size, and with a scale of feet attached, to accompany the Farm Book, so that the land may be laid out in a winter evening.

Areas warranted accurate within almost any degree of exactness, and the Variation of the Compass given, so that the lines can be run again. Apply to

HENRY D. THOREAU.

This map of Walden Pond was created by Thoreau, who was a gifted land surveyor. Surveying involves precisely measuring the distance between two points on land and is generally used for mapmaking and determining property boundaries. Many of Thoreau's surveys still exist, as do the handbills *(inset)* that he used to advertise his business.

'civilized off the face of the earth,'–our forests, not to hold the king's game merely, but to hold and preserve the king himself also, the lord of creation,–not for idle sport or food, but for inspiration and our own true re-creation?

As a protector of the land, Thoreau was far ahead of his time. Thanks to his work and efforts of people like him, the U.S. government created the National Park Service (NPS) in 1916. With more than 50 million acres (214.7 ha) spread across 60 parks in the United States, the NPS has become an important part of America's conservation effort. It works to preserve natural resources and save the nation's forests for future generations.

On the slopes of Mount Katahdin, Thoreau left his fellow travelers behind and scrambled over the rocks and bushes to the rocky summit covered in fog. Standing alone near the top, Thoreau experienced nature in a new way.

It was not lawn, nor pasture, nor mead, nor woodland, nor lea, nor arable, nor waste-land. It was the fresh and natural surface of the planet Earth, as it was made for ever and ever,–to be the dwelling of man, we say,–so Nature made it, and man may use it if he can . . . There was there felt the presence of a force not bound to be kind to man . . . What is it to be admitted to a museum,

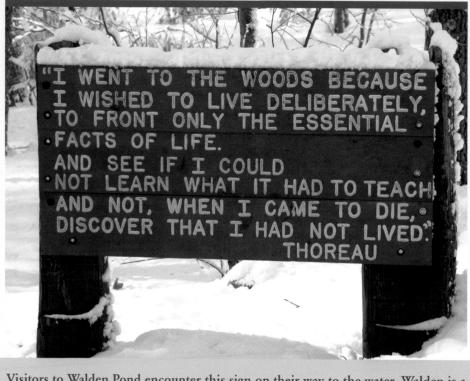

"I WENT TO THE WOODS BECAUSE I WISHED TO LIVE DELIBERATELY, TO FRONT ONLY THE ESSENTIAL FACTS OF LIFE. AND SEE IF I COULD NOT LEARN WHAT IT HAD TO TEACH AND NOT, WHEN I CAME TO DIE, DISCOVER THAT I HAD NOT LIVED."
THOREAU

Visitors to Walden Pond encounter this sign on their way to the water. Walden is a popular swimming and hiking destination, and it has been declared a National Historic Landmark. Visitors come from all over the world to take in the beauty of the pond and the surrounding woods.

to see a myriad of particular things, compared with being shown some star's surface, some hard matter in its home!

In all of his walks, in his many trips short and long, Thoreau had never seen the natural world outside of man's influence. It was nature in pursuit of itself, presenting itself exactly as it was. Standing near the summit of the highest mountain in New England, Thoreau had reached the zenith of his explorations in nature, for he would never again find himself so wonderfully and joyfully removed from the world of man.

CHAPTER
5

THOREAU'S LEGACY

In the winter of 1860, Thoreau caught a cold. Thoreau had been plagued by symptoms of tuberculosis throughout most of his adult life, and the cold worsened quickly. Rather than rest his weakened body, he agreed to speak at the lyceum in Waterbury, Connecticut. As a result of the travel, the lecture, and the trip back, Thoreau found that his cold deepened into bronchitis. Through the rest of the winter, his condition worsened, and the painful cough in his sickly lungs did not go away. In May 1861, Thoreau managed to visit Minnesota to study its plants, but the trip was

Mohandas Gandhi, shown here addressing a crowd in India in 1931, was one of the greatest civil rights leaders of the twentieth century. Under his leadership, India broke free from British colonial rule. Gandhi advocated a form of nonviolent civil disobedience that he called *satyagraha*, an Indian word meaning "devotion to the truth."

cut short due to his poor health. After a short trip in August, Thoreau returned to Concord, never to leave again.

Thoreau sensed that the end was near and began to prepare his papers for history. He corrected mistakes that had occurred during the printing of his two published books: *A Week on the Concord and Merrimack Rivers* and *Walden*. In late September, he made a final visit to Walden Pond. On November 3, 1861, he made his final entry into the journal to which he had been devoted for twenty-four years. "All this is perfectly distinct to an observant eye, and yet could easily pass unnoticed by most." Confined to his home for much of the following spring, he tried to scrape off the ice on the windows to see the outside world. When his energy

Thoreau is buried in Sleepy Hollow Cemetery in Concord, Massachusetts. The cemetery also contains the graves of authors such as Louisa May Alcott and Nathaniel Hawthorne. Thoreau's longtime friend and mentor Ralph Waldo Emerson is also buried in the cemetery.

allowed, he continued to work on his unfinished collection of narratives, *The Maine Woods*, and manuscripts that he submitted for publication. In the evening of May 6, 1862, his faint breath just faded away.

At the time of his death, Thoreau was barely known outside of Concord. He had published one book (*A Week on the Concord and Merrimack Rivers*) with his own money, and more than 700 copies out of one thousand had failed to sell. His other book, *Walden*, had received favorable reviews, but some dismissed it as a call to return to the woods. Beyond his two unsuccessful books and a few magazine articles, he had not accomplished much as a published writer in his own lifetime. As Emerson noted in his speech at Thoreau's funeral, according to the Works of Ralph Waldo Emerson Web site:

> I so much regret the loss of his rare powers of action, that I cannot help counting it a fault in him that he had no ambition. Wanting this [lacking ambition] instead of engineering for all America, he was the captain of a huckleberry party. Pounding beans is good to the end of pounding empires one of these days; but if, at the end of years, it is still only beans!

Like many of the great writers in history, Thoreau's time was not his own; it would take nearly a century before scholars,

The civil rights movement in the United States was spearheaded by Dr. Martin Luther King Jr. Shown here holding the arm of his wife, Coretta Scott King, at the head of a voting rights march in Alabama, Dr. King won a Nobel Peace Prize in 1964 for his work fighting racial injustice. Thoreau's writing greatly influenced Dr. King, whose philosophy of nonviolent resistance made him a hero to people all over the world. He was assassinated on April 4, 1968, in Memphis, Tennessee.

writers, political activists, and rebels of various sorts realized his gifts to humankind.

COINCIDENCE AND OPPORTUNITY

A rare set of coincidences led to the written works Thoreau left for humankind. If Emerson had not suffered tragic loss in his life, he may not have left his comfortable life in Boston to travel to Europe. If he had not gone to Europe, he would not have met Carlyle and Coleridge. If he had not met them, he may not have returned with a new philosophical outlook. If he had not embraced transcendentalism and advanced it in America, those ideas may not have been planted so firmly in the mind of his younger neighbor, whose personality, interests, and intellectual abilities led him to produce works of art that have influenced millions. Yet, Thoreau's gifts to humankind were made possible by these two men doing what came most naturally to them—following their inner light.

Although it was dismantled after he moved out, a replica of Thoreau's cabin stands at Walden Pond. A bronze statue of the author is situated not far from the cabin. Visitors to the site can get an idea of what Thoreau's time there might have been like.

In the middle of the nineteenth century, only in America was the true flowering of transcendentalism possible. In Great Britain, which produced Carlyle and Coleridge, the tradition of kings, queens, dukes, and lords ensured that all men were not created equal. In Germany, where transcendentalism was born, the land was split into dozens of independent states, in which nearby neighbors were living under different laws. In those places, the importance of the individual, whether he or she was a laborer or emperor, was unable to flourish.

America, however, was the land of opportunity and experimentation, and millions were drawn to it. In America, traditions were distrusted, as most Americans linked them with the European rulers whom they or their ancestors had fled. In America, people were willing to experiment with new ideas and live vibrant lives across the unblemished canvas of an entire continent.

Only in America was the nation's first document, the Declaration of Independence, bold enough to declare that "all men are created equal," and that each one had the inalienable right to "Life, Liberty and the pursuit of Happiness." Although the Declaration of Independence stated that these two ideas were important, it was Thoreau, among others, who told us why. By pursuing his life as he defined it, separating himself from society and finding happiness in the natural world, Thoreau realized all life was precious. He believed that all humans, plants, and animals are created equal under the higher law that he saw contained in each of us.

WHAT HE LEAVES US

In the middle of the nineteenth century, America made room for Henry David Thoreau, an individual whose basic instinct was to follow a different life-path from most people. Along the way, his discoveries in himself and in the natural world advanced the cause of civil rights, the values of simplicity, and the importance of conservation. He even made contributions to natural history. Later in life, he was asked to join the Association for the Advancement of Science. Thoreau noted the following in his journal:

> I felt that it would be to make myself the laughing-stock of the scientific community to describe or attempt to describe to them that branch of science in which specially interests me, inasmuch as they do not believe in a science which deals with the higher law . . . The fact is I am a mystic, a transcendentalist, and a natural philosopher to boot. Now that I think of it, I should have told them at once that I was a transcendentalist. That would have been the shortest way of telling that they would not understand my explanations.

Thoreau is considered to be one of the first advocates of nature conservation and an early practitioner of ecology, or the study of the interaction between organisms and their environments. Although Thoreau has come to be regarded as one of America's greatest writers, he was not appreciated in his time. In the conclusion to *Walden*, he famously wrote, "If a man does not keep pace with his companions, perhaps it is because he hears a different drummer."

True to his word, Thoreau did not join the group. Although his opinions were often unpopular even with his closest friends, he stood by them, in public speeches, in private writings in his journal, and in the life he lived.

Yet this man whose reach has extended across history, economy, language, botany, conservation, and civil rights found most of his inspiration in the area around the small town of Concord, Massachusetts. He was born and lived right where he needed to be: at the border between civilization and nature in the grand experiment of America. It was here that Thoreau scattered the seeds of his ideas, which would survive through history to flower across the entire world. As quoted on the Works of Ralph Waldo Emerson Web site, Emerson noted at Thoreau's funeral: "He had a beautiful soul, he had a beautiful soul."

TIMELINE

1817 Thoreau is born in Concord, Massachusetts, on July 12.

1828 Thoreau writes his essay "The Seasons."

1833 Thoreau enrolls at Harvard College after barely passing the entrance exams.

1836 Ralph Waldo Emerson first expresses the ideas of transcendentalism in his essay "Nature." Thoreau is greatly influenced by Emerson's work.

1837 Thoreau graduates from Harvard College. He begins a journal on October 22. Thoreau and Emerson become friends in the fall. Thoreau attends meetings of the Hedge Club at Emerson's house—a regular gathering of what newspapers later called the transcendentalists.

1838 Thoreau is elected secretary and curator of the Concord Lyceum and serves in both offices until December 1840.

1839 Thoreau and his brother, John, make an excursion on the Concord and Merrimack rivers. Emerson founds the *Dial* with other transcendentalists.

1842 John Thoreau dies on January 11 from lockjaw.

1844 Thoreau contributes articles to the last volume of the *Dial*, released in April.

1845 Thoreau moves to his cabin at Walden Pond on July 4 and stays for two winters.

1846 Thoreau is arrested and jailed overnight for nonpayment of taxes. He makes his first trip to the Maine woods.

1848 Thoreau's article "Katahdin and the Maine Woods" is published in *Union* magazine.

1849 Thoreau publishes *A Week on the Concord and Merrimack Rivers* and "Resistance to Civil Government" ("Civil Disobedience") in *Aesthetic Papers*. He makes his his first trip to Cape Cod.

1854 Thoreau's *Walden* is published. His lecture "Slavery in Massachusetts" is delivered in Framingham; the lecture is published in the *Liberator*.

1855 Thoreau visits Cape Cod; portions of "Cape Cod" are published in *Putnam's* magazine.

1857 Thoreau visits Cape Cod and the Maine woods; he meets John Brown.

1859 Thoreau's father dies on February 3. He lectures on "A Plea for Captain John Brown" and "After the Death of John Brown."

1860 "A Plea for Captain John Brown" is published in *Echoes of Harpers Ferry*; "The Last Days of John Brown" appears in the *Liberator*. Thoreau delivers "The Succession

(continued on following page)

(continued from previous page)

of Forest Trees" as a lecture at the Middlesex Cattle Show, later published in *Transactions of the Middlesex Agricultural Society*.

1862 Henry David Thoreau dies on May 6.

GLOSSARY

abolitionist One who seeks to abolish something. In American history, abolitionists sought to end slavery.

botany The study of plants.

civil disobedience A form of nonviolent protest in which people refuse to obey laws that they consider to be unjust.

ecology The study of the relationship between plants, animals, and their environment.

lyceum An organization that sponsors educational programs and entertainment for the public at little or no cost. The lyceum movement in America began in the 1820s.

phenomena Things that can be observed or experienced through the five senses: sight, hearing, smell, taste, and touch.

poll tax A tax placed on an individual for the right to vote. Poll taxes are no longer allowed in the United States.

rationality The quality of having good sense and judgment. Often, rationality is linked to the use of logic.

reformer One who strives to make changes in society.

transcendentalism A movement in literature and philosophy that advances the idea of a spiritual reality that is not knowable by science and observation. Transcendentalists look within themselves for spiritual guidance.

tuberculosis A lung disease caused by bacteria; also known as TB or consumption.

Unitarianism A religious belief in one God, but not the idea of the Holy Trinity: Father, Son, and Holy Spirit. Unitarians believe in freedom of the individual to find God within himself or herself.

FOR MORE INFORMATION

The Concord Museum
200 Lexington Road
Concord, MA 01742
(978) 369-9763
Web site: http://www.concordmuseum.org

Northern Illinois University
The Writings of Henry David Thoreau–Thoreau Edition
Founders Memorial Library
Northern Illinois University
DeKalb, IL 60115-2868
(815) 753-1849
Web site: http://www.thoreau.niu.edu

Walden Pond State Reservation
915 Walden Street
Concord, MA 01742
(978) 369-3254
Web site: http://www.mass.gov/dcr/parks/northeast/
  wldn.htm

The Walden Woods Project
44 Baker Farm Road
Lincoln, MA 01773-3004
(781) 259-4700
Web site: http://www.walden.org

WEB SITES

Due to the changing nature of Internet links, the Rosen Publishing Group, Inc., has developed an online list of Web sites related to the subject of this book. This site is updated regularly. Please use this link to access the list:

http://www.rosenlinks.com/lat/heth

For Further Reading

Anderson, Peter. *Henry David Thoreau: American Naturalist.* New York, NY: Franklin Watts, 1995.

Bloom, Harold. *Henry David Thoreau.* Philadelphia, PA: Chelsea House Publishers, 2003.

Dawes, Claiborne. *A Different Drummer: Thoreau and Will's Independence Day.* Carlisle, MA: Discovery Enterprises Ltd., 1998.

McCarthy, Pat. *Henry David Thoreau: Writer, Thinker, Naturalist.* Berkeley Heights, NJ: Enslow Publishers, 2003.

Murphy, Jim. *Into the Deep Forest with Henry David Thoreau.* New York, NY: Clarion Books, 1995.

Reef, Catherine. *Henry David Thoreau: A Neighbor to Nature.* Frederick, MD: Twenty-first Century Books, 1991.

Stern, Philip Van Doren. *Henry David Thoreau: Writer and Rebel.* New York, NY: Ty Crowell Company, 1972.

Thoreau, Henry David. *Cape Cod.* New York, NY: HarperCollins Children's Books, 1972.

Thoreau, Henry David. *New Suns Will Arise: From the Journals of Henry David Thoreau*. Edited by Frank Crocitto. New York, NY: Hyperion, 2000.

Thoreau, Henry David. *Walden and Resistance to Civil Government*. Edited by William Rossi. New York, NY: W. W. Norton and Company, 1992.

BIBLIOGRAPHY

"Concord River." Lowell Parks & Conservation Trust. Retrieved January 26, 2005 (http://lowelllandtrust.org/Concord_river.html).

"The Declaration of Independence: A Transcription." National Archives Experience. Retrieved February 22, 2005 (http://www.archives.gov/national_archives_experience/charters/declaration_transcript.html).

Emerson, Ralph Waldo. "The American Scholar." Ralph Waldo Emerson Texts. Retrieved March 23, 2005 (http://www.emersoncentral.com/amscholar.htm).

Emerson, Ralph Waldo. "The Eulogy of Henry David Thoreau." RWE.org—The Works of Ralph Waldo Emerson. Retrieved January 29, 2005 (http://www.rwe.org/pages/eulogy_of_thoreau.htm).

"Era of Good Feeling." Wikipedia. December 2, 2004. Retrieved January 26, 2005 (http://en.wikipedia.org/wiki/Era_of_Good_Feeling).

Foerster, Norman. *The Intellectual Heritage of Thoreau.* Folcroft, PA: Folcroft Library Editions, 1974.

"German Idealism." Internet Encyclopedia of Philosophy.
  2001. Retrieved January 28, 2005 (http://www.utm.edu/
  research/iep/g/germidea.htm).
Harding, Walter. *The Days of Henry Thoreau.* New York, NY:
  Alfred A. Knopf, 1965.
Harding, Walter, and Michael Meyer. *The New Thoreau
  Handbook.* New York, NY: New York University Press, 1980.
"Henry David Thoreau." Wikipedia. November 23, 2004.
  Retrieved November 28, 2004 (http://en.wikipedia.org/
  wiki/Thoreau).
Hileman, Bryan C. "Ralph Waldo Emerson: Emerson and
  Thomas Carlyle." American Transcendentalism Web. June
  18, 2003. Retrieved January 27, 2005 (http://www.vcu.edu/
  engweb/transcendentalism/roots/rwe-tc.html).
Hileman, Bryan C. "Transcendental Roots: Emerson and
  Coleridge." American Transcendentalism Web. June 18,
  2003. Retrieved January 27, 2005 (http://www.vcu.edu/
  engweb/transcendentalism/roots/rwe-cole.html).
Hileman, Bryan C. "Transcendental Roots: Emerson and
  Immanuel Kant." American Transcendentalism Web.
  June 18, 2003. Retrieved January 28, 2005 (http://
  www.vcu.edu/engweb/transcendentalism/roots/
  rwe-kant.html).
King, Martin Luther, Jr. *The Autobiography of Martin Luther
  King, Jr.* Edited by Clayborne Carson. New York, NY:
  IPM/Warner Books, 1998.

Lebeaux, Richard. *Thoreau's Seasons.* Amherst, MA:
University of Massachusetts Press, 1984.

Lebeaux, Richard. *Young Man Thoreau.* Amherst, MA:
University of Massachusetts Press, 1977.

"Lecture 2." Thoreau Institute of Walden Woods. With
permission from Joel Myerson and Ronald Wesley Hoag.
2004. Retrieved February 2, 2005 (http://www.walden.org/
institute/thoreau/life/Lecturing/02_Lecture.htm).

Meltzer, Milton, ed. *Thoreau: People, Principles and Politics.*
New York, NY: Hill & Wang, 1963.

"National Parks." InfoPlease. 2005. Retrieved February 26,
2005 (http://www.infoplease.com/ipa/A0884500.html).

"New England Transcendentalism, Ralph Waldo Emerson and
Kantian or Transcendental Idealism." The Age of the Sage.
October 2002. Retrieved January 28, 2005 (http://www.
age-of-the-sage.org/transcendentalism/emerson/idealism_
kant.html#Emerson_Kantian_Transcendental_Idealism).

"Ralph Waldo Emerson." Wikipedia. November 18, 2004.
Retrieved November 28, 2004 (http://en.wikipedia.org/
wiki/Emerson).

Richardson, Robert D., Jr. "Ralph Waldo Emerson." *Dictionary
of Literary Biography, Volume 59: American Literary Critics and
Scholars, 1800–1850.* Detroit, MI: Gale Research, 1987.

"Samuel Taylor Coleridge." Wikipedia. January 25, 2005.
Retrieved January 26, 2005 (http://en.wikipedia.org/wiki/
Coleridge).

Schneider, Richard J. *Henry David Thoreau*. Boston, MA: Twayne Publishers, 1987.

Stokes, Philip. *Philosophy: 100 Essential Thinkers*. New York, NY: Enchanted Lion Books, 2003.

"Thomas Carlyle." Wikipedia. January 22, 2005. Retrieved January 26, 2005 (http://en.wikipedia.org/wiki/Thomas_Carlyle).

Thoreau, Henry David. "Civil Disobedience." The Thoreau Reader. February 19, 2005. Retrieved February 22, 2005 (http://eserver.org/thoreau/civil1.html).

Thoreau, Henry David. "Natural History of Massachusetts." Transcribed by Bradley Dean from 1906 Houghton Mifflin edition. American Transcendentalism Web. June 18, 2003. Retrieved February 16, 2005 (http://www.vcu.edu/engweb/transcendentalism/authors/thoreau/nathist.html).

Thoreau, Henry David. "A Plea for Captain John Brown." Project Gutenberg. March 2001. Retrieved February 23, 2005 (http://www.gutenberg.org/dirs/etext01/apcjb10.txt).

Thoreau, Henry David. *Walden and Civil Disobedience*. Belmont, CA: Wadsworth, 2004.

INDEX

About the Author

Steven P. Olson is a writer who lives in Oakland, California, and enjoys traveling the world. His travels have taken him to Concord, Massachusetts, and Walden Pond, which sparked his interest in writing this book.

Photo Credits:

Cover portrait, pp. 1, 7, 12, 16, 18, 19, 31, 33, 35, 42, 49, 51, 53, 57, 69, 80 Concord Free Public Library; cover (background) © Bill Ross/Corbis; pp. 9, 74, 89 © Getty Images; p. 15 © Kevin Fleming/Corbis; pp. 21, 25, 85 © Bettmann/Corbis; p. 23 Scala/Art Resource, NY; pp. 38–39 The Piermont Morgan Library/Art Resource, NY; pp. 45, 59 Library of Congress Prints and Photographs Division; p. 61 The Huntington Library, San Marino, CA; p. 67 © North Wind Picture Archives; p. 78 © Yogi, Inc./Corbis; p. 80 (inset) Henry W. and Albert A. Berg Collection of English and American Literature, The New York Public Library, Astor, Lenox and Tilden Foundations; p. 82 © Tom Brosnahan; pp. 86–87 © Ed Young/Corbis; p. 91 © AP/Wide World Photos; p. 94 © David Muench/Corbis.

Designer: Gene Mollica
Photo Researcher: Marty Levick